# ANIMALS

# Whales

**by Kevin J. Holmes**

*Content Consultant*:
**Phil Clapham, Ph.D.**
**Smithsonian Institute**

## Bridgestone Books

an imprint of Capstone Press

Bridgestone Books are published by Capstone Press,
151 Good Counsel Drive, P.O. Box 669, Mankato, Minnesota 56002.
www.capstonepress.com

*Library of Congress Cataloging-in-Publication Data*
Holmes, Kevin J.
    Whales/by Kevin J. Holmes.
    p. cm. -- (Animals)
    Includes bibliographical references (p. 23) and index.
    Summary:  An introduction to whales, covering their physical characteristics,
habits, prey, and relationship to humans.
    ISBN 1-56065-601-8 (hardcover)
    ISBN 0-7368-8073-9 (paperback)
    1. Whales--Juvenile literature. [1. Whales.]
    I. Title.  II. Series:  Animals (Mankato, Minn.)
QL737.C4H655   1998
599.5--dc21

        97-8240
        CIP
        AC

**Editorial credits**
Editor, Timothy Larson; Cover design, Timothy Halldin; Photo Research Assistant,
  Michelle L. Norstad

**Photo credits**
Innerspace Visions/James D. Watt, 6; Doug Perrine, cover, 8, 12, 16, 18;
  Michael Nolan, 10
Unicorn Stock/Marcia Pennington, 14
Visuals Unlimited, 20

3  4  5  6  7  10  09  08  07  06

# Table of Contents

Dorsal Fin

Blowhole

Fluke

Flippers

# Fast Facts

**Kinds:**  All whales are either toothed whales or baleen whales. Toothed whales have teeth. Baleen whales have no teeth.

**Range:**  Whales live in all the oceans of the world.

**Habitat:**  Whales live in coastal and deep ocean waters. Many whales move to cooler ocean waters in the summer. These whales return to warmer ocean waters in the winter.

**Food:**  Toothed whales eat fish and squid. A squid is a sea animal with a long, soft body. A squid has 10 arms called tentacles. Baleen whales eat fish and krill. Krill are tiny shrimp.

**Young:**  Young whales are called calves. Each female whale usually gives birth to one calf. Female whales give birth every one to five years.

# Whales

Whales are sea mammals. A mammal is a warm-blooded animal with a backbone. Warm-blooded means having a set body temperature. Mammals also breathe air and give birth to live young.

All whales are cetaceans. Cetaceans are a group of sea mammals. The cetacean group also includes dolphins and porpoises. Whales and other cetaceans live in the oceans of the world.

There are about 80 different species of whales. A species is a group of animals with shared features. Animals in the same species can join together to produce young.

Scientists put whale species into two larger groups. Species in the first group have teeth. These are called toothed whales. Species in the second group have baleen instead of teeth. These are called baleen whales. Baleen is rows of long, thin bone. Baleen hangs from the upper jaw inside the mouth.

**Whales are sea mammals.**

# Appearance

Whales have large, fish-like bodies. They have wide, flat arms called flippers. They have one flipper on each side of their bodies. Whales have tails called flukes. Some whales also have small fins on the tops of their backs. These are called dorsal fins. Their flippers, tails, and fins help them swim.

Whales have eyes on the sides of their heads. They also have blowholes on top of their heads. A blowhole is a hole that works like a nose. Whales breathe through their blowholes.

Whale bodies are covered with skin. A thick layer of blubber lies beneath their skin. Blubber is fat. It helps keep whales warm in cold water. Blubber also gives whales energy when they have no food. It helps whales float in the water, too.

Different species of whales are different colors. Some are blue-gray. Some are just gray. Others are white. Still others are black and white.

**Whales have large, fish-like bodies.**

# Where Whales Live

Whales live in coastal and deep ocean waters. They can be found in all oceans of the world. Many whale species migrate in summer and winter. Migrate means to move from one place to another. Some species do not migrate.

In the summer, many whale species migrate to cold water areas. Some cold water areas are close to the North Pole. Other areas are close to the South Pole. The whales migrate to cold water to find food.

In the winter, many whale species migrate to warm water areas. These areas are near the Earth's equator. The equator is an imaginary line. It divides the Earth into northern and southern halves. Whales move to warm water to have their young.

Most whale species live in both sides of the equator. Some live only in the northern side. Other species live only in the southern side.

**Whales live in coastal and deep ocean waters.**

# How Whales Act

Whales must be on top of the water to breathe. They breathe by sucking air into their lungs through their blowholes. Whales blow old air out of their lungs through their blowholes. They take several breaths before they dive.

Whales dive deep below the surface of the water. Some whales can dive more than 6,700 feet (2,000 meters). Many whales can stay underwater for more than 75 minutes. All whales return to the surface to breathe.

Whales are also active on the top of the water. Some jump out of the water. This is called breaching. Some wave their flippers. Others slap their flukes on the surface of the water. This is called lob tailing.

No one knows if whales sleep like people sleep. Scientists think that whales only rest. They think whales rest on or near the water's surface. Otherwise, whales would not be able to breathe.

**Some whales slap their flukes on the water.**

# What Whales Eat

Toothed whales and baleen whales eat different things. Toothed whales eat fish, shrimp, and squid. A squid is a sea animal with a long, soft body. A squid has 10 arms called tentacles.

Toothed whales use their teeth to catch their food. They do not chew their food. They swallow it whole. Some toothed whales can swallow large squid. The squid are up to 40 feet (12 meters) long.

Baleen whales eat krill and small fish. Krill are tiny shrimp. Baleen whales eat by taking large mouthfuls of krill or fish. The animals become trapped in the whales' baleen. Baleen whales are then able to swallow the krill and fish.

Baleen whales need to eat a lot. They are large animals, but their food is small. Baleen whales eat up to six tons (about five and one-half metric tons) of food each day.

**Baleen whales need to eat a lot.**

# Enemies

Whales have few natural enemies. Sometimes sharks attack whales and whale young. Killer whales also attack small whales and their young. Killer whales are a species of toothed whales.

People are the greatest enemies of whales. In the past, people hunted whales. They killed whales for food. They also killed whales for their blubber. The blubber was made into oil for soap and candles.

People also polluted the oceans. Polluted water killed the food whales eat. It also made some whales sick and killed young whales.

Hunting and pollution lowered the number of whales. Some whale species almost became extinct. Extinct means no longer living or existing.

Soon, people saw they had to protect whales. They passed laws. The laws stopped most whale hunting. They stopped some pollution. Today, most whales are protected by laws.

**Killer whales attack whales and their young.**

# Young Whales

Each female whale usually gives birth to one calf. A calf is a young whale. Some female whales give birth every one to three years. Others give birth every five years or more.

Female whales make milk in their bodies. They feed the milk to their calves. The milk helps calves grow quickly. Calves gain up to 200 pounds (90 kilograms) each day. Some calves grow as much as one inch (about two and one-half centimeters) per day.

Some calves stay with their mothers up to one year. These calves then set out on their own. They stay on their own until it is time to produce young. Other young whales become part of pods. A pod is a group of whales.

Whales live a long time. How long whales live is different for each species. Some toothed whales live about 30 years. Other toothed whales live up to 80 years. Most baleen whales live 50 to 100 years.

**Each female whale usually gives birth to one calf.**

# Kinds of Whales

Blue and humpback whales are some of the best known baleen whales. Narwhal and killer whales are well known toothed whales.

Blue whales are named for their blue-gray color. They can grow over 100 feet (30 meters) long. Blue whales weigh as much as 200 tons (180 metric tons).

Each humpback whale has a hump near its dorsal fin. People named humpbacks for this hump. Humpbacks are gray or black with white undersides. They grow up to 60 feet (18 meters) long. Humpbacks weigh as much as 45 tons (41 metric tons).

Narwhals have a mixture of white and gray spots. Male narwhals grow tusks up to 10 feet (three meters) long. A tusk is a long tooth.

Killer whales are black and white. They grow up to 33 feet (10 meters) long. Killer whales are usually gentle around each other and humans. But they will hunt smaller whales and other sea mammals.

**Male narwhals have tusks.**

# Hands On: Measure Whales

Some whales are very large. They are so large it is hard to imagine their size. This activity will help you see the size of two whales.

## What You Need

One tape measure (at least 100 feet or 30 meters long)
One set of colored chalk
An adult to help you measure
A couple of friends

## What You Do

1. Measure out the length of a blue whale. Use the tape measure to do this. A blue whale is about 100 feet (30 meters) long.
2. Mark the beginning and end of the length in chalk. Use one color of chalk to do this.
3. Repeat the steps for the humpback whale. A humpback whale is 60 feet (18 meters) long.
4. Have your friends lay down along your chalk lines. How many friends equal the length of each whale?
5. You can repeat these steps for other whales, too.

# Words to Know

**baleen** (bay-LEEN)—rows of long, thin bone; baleen whales have baleen instead of teeth

**equator** (i-KWAY-tur)—an imaginary line that divides the Earth into northern and southern halves

**fluke** (FLOOK)—a whale's tail

**krill** (KRIL)—tiny shrimp

**mammal** (MAM-uhl)—a warm-blooded animal with a backbone

**pod** (POD)—a group of whales

# Read More

**Clapham, Phil**. *Whales of the World*. Stillwater, Minn.: Voyageur Press, 1997.

**Corrigan, Patricia**. *Whales*. Our Wild World. Minnetonka, Minn.: NorthWord Press, 2001.

**Greenaway, Theresa**. *Whales*. The Secret World of. Austin, Texas: Raintree Steck-Vaughn, 2001.

## Useful Addresses

**American Cetacean Society**
P.O. Box 1391
San Pedro, CA  90733

**Save the Whales**
P.O. Box 2397
Venice, CA  90291

## Internet Sites

FactHound offers a safe, fun way to find Internet sites related to this book.

Go to *www.facthound.com*

He'll fetch the best sites for you!

## Index